BBC earth

DO YOU KNOW?

Level 2

ANIMALS AT NIGHT

Inspired by BBC Earth TV series and developed with input from BBC Earth natural history specialists

Written by Sarah Wassner-Flynn
Text adapted by Nick Coates
Series Editor: Nick Coates

LADYBIRD BOOKS

UK | USA | Canada | Ireland | Australia
India | New Zealand | South Africa

Ladybird Books is part of the Penguin Random House group of companies
whose addresses can be found at global.penguinrandomhouse.com.
www.penguin.co.uk   www.puffin.co.uk   www.ladybird.co.uk

Penguin
Random House
UK

First published 2020
001

Printed in China

A CIP catalogue record for this book is available from the British Library

ISBN: 978-0-241-35582-4

All correspondence to:
Ladybird Books Ltd
Penguin Random House Children's
One Embassy Gardens, New Union Square
5 Nine Elms Lane, London SW8 5DA

Contents

New words

bottom

climb
(verb)

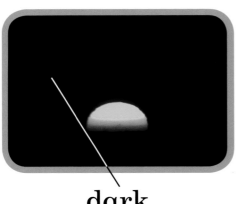

dark
(noun)

desert

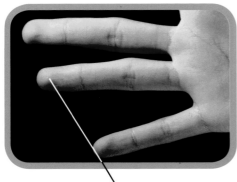

finger

forest

grass

insect

light
(noun)

rubbish bin

sand

smell
(noun and verb)

upside down

Do animals sleep at night?

Do you sleep in the day or at night?

Many animals sleep at night. They wake up in the morning.

Sifaka lemurs wake up with the sun.

Some animals don't sleep at night. They are called nocturnal animals.

Bats are nocturnal.

Nocturnal animals sleep in the day.

These animals are nocturnal, too.

WATCH!

Watch the video (see page 32).
Why do the leopards go into the city at night?
Can the other animals see them?

When do lions eat?

Lions sleep in the day.

It is hot in the sun.

It is too hot to run.

In the evening,
it isn't hot.

It is time
for the lions
to look for food.

It is time to eat!

The lions can
see very well
at night.

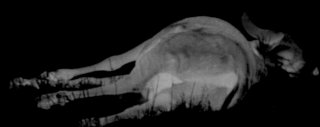

They can see
other animals
in the **dark**.

 THINK!

Lions can see other animals.
Can the other animals see
the lions? Why? Why not?

9

What do skunks do at night?

Skunks sleep all day as well. They look for food at night.

Skunks eat food like **grass** and **insects**.

A skunk uses its nose to find food.

A skunk doesn't like
some animals.

It makes a horrible **smell**.

The other animals
don't like the smell.
They go away.

FIND OUT!

Use books or the internet
to find out where skunks live.

Where do raccoons live?

Some raccoons live in **forests**. Some live in towns and cities.

Raccoons in cities find food in **rubbish bins**.

At night, they go to people's homes.

Raccoons can **climb** very well.

They open the rubbish bins.
Then they climb in to find food!

This raccoon finds a birdhouse.
It looks for food inside.

▶ WATCH!

**Watch the video
(see page 32).**
What body parts do
raccoons use to climb?

What is an aye-aye?

It is night
in the forest.
An aye-aye
wakes up.

In the day,
it sleeps in
a warm bed
in a tree.

But now it
wants to eat!

An aye-aye is an animal with big eyes, big ears and long **fingers**.

It can hold insects with its fingers.

The aye-aye can see well at night. It can see and hear the insects it likes to eat.

LOOK!

Look at the pages.
What helps the aye-aye find food at night?

How do bats find food?

In the day, bats sleep **upside down**.

Bats can see at night. They can hear very well, too.

At night, they
fly to find food.

One bat can eat
many insects in
one night.

The desert long-eared
bat uses its ears to find
insects at night.

Some bats eat insects.
Some eat fruit.

PROJECT

Work in a group.
Use books or the internet to find as many different types
of bat as you can. Choose one and draw a picture of it.
Label its eyes, ears, nose, wings and legs.

Where do fennec foxes sleep?

This fennec fox lives in the **desert**.

The desert is too hot in the day for the fox.

It sleeps in a bed under the **sand**.

The fennec fox has very big ears to help it find food in the dark.

At night, it goes out in the desert.

THINK!

Why do fennec foxes sleep under the sand?

19

Why are there a lot of insects at night?

There are more insects at night than in the day.

Many animals and birds eat insects in the day.

Insects walk or fly at night because many animals and birds are sleeping.

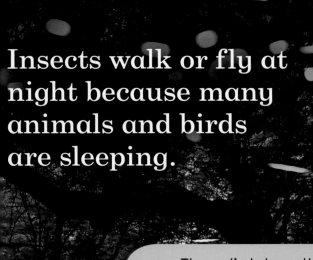

lights

The click beetle has **lights** on its head.

Fireflies have lights, too.

 FIND OUT!

Use books or the internet to find two things that an insect eats.

When do sharks sleep?

Some fish and sea animals sleep in the sea at night.

But some don't! That is when they look for food.

These are nocturnal sea animals.

Some sharks have to swim all the time.
They never stop. They don't sleep!

They find food in the
dark because they
can see and hear
very well.

This great white shark
swims all night. It is looking
for something to eat.

THINK!

Would you like to stay awake all
night? What would you do?

How do fish see in the sea?

Down at the **bottom** of the sea, it is always dark.

The fish and sea animals never see the day!

They can find food because they have big eyes.

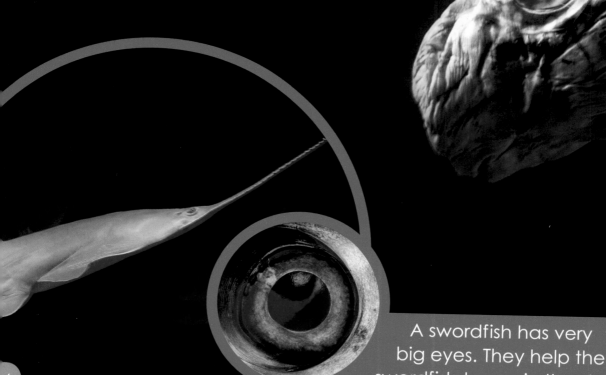

A swordfish has very big eyes. They help the swordfish to see in the dark.

4

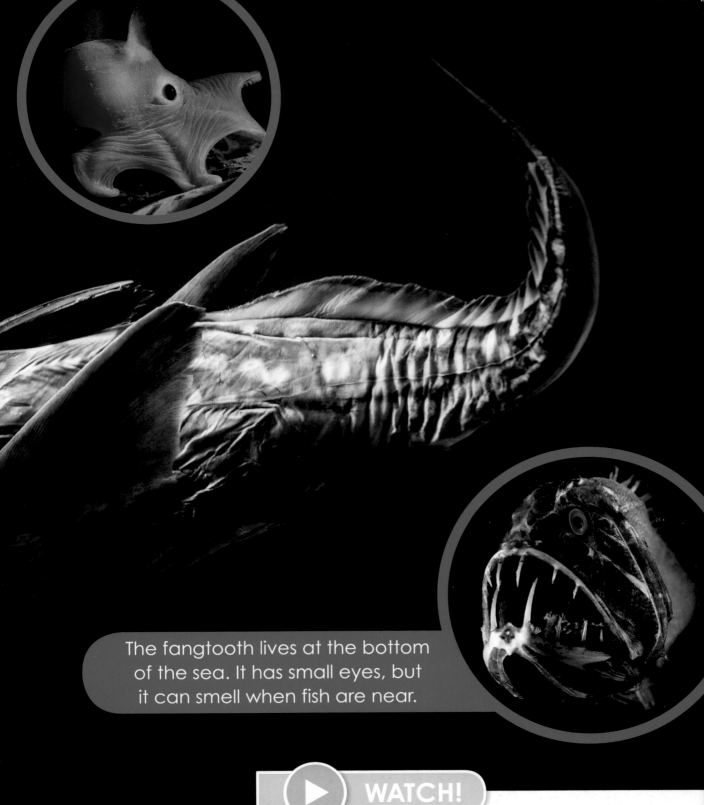

The fangtooth lives at the bottom of the sea. It has small eyes, but it can smell when fish are near.

WATCH!

Watch the video (see page 32).
What other part of the swordfish is interesting and unusual, do you think?

What is that noise?

Frogs make a lot of noise at night.
Many frogs are nocturnal.
They talk to other frogs.

Sometimes they are saying,
"I like you. Come here."

Red-eyed tree frogs are nocturnal.

But sometimes they are saying, "I don't like you. Go away."

LOOK!

Look at the pages.
What are the two main reasons that frogs make noise?

What do hippos do at night?

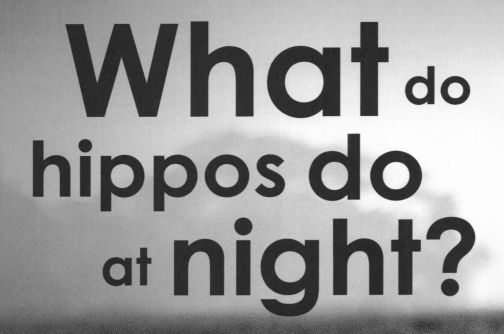

Hippos live in hot places.

In the day, when it is very hot, they stay in the river.

The water is not hot.

They swim, play and sleep.

At night, the hippos leave the river to eat.

They eat grass for six hours. Then they go back to the river.

LOOK!

Look at the pages.
What do the hippos do when they leave the river?

Quiz

Choose the correct answers.

1 Nocturnal animals . . .
   a sleep at night.
   b sleep in the day.
   c never sleep.

2 Which animal is NOT nocturnal?
   a a bat
   b a raccoon
   c a sifaka lemur

3 A skunk finds food with its . . .
   a nose.
   b eyes.
   c ears.

4 An aye-aye does NOT have . . .
   a big ears.
   b big eyes.
   c long legs.

5 A fennec fox lives in the . . .
   a city.
   b desert.
   c forest.

6 Some sharks . . .
   a never sleep.
   b never eat.
   c always sleep.

7 Hippos eat . . .
   a fish.
   b grass.
   c insects.

Visit www.ladybirdeducation.co.uk for FREE DO YOU KNOW? teaching resources.

- video clips with simplified voiceover and subtitles
- video and comprehension activities
- class projects and lesson plans
- audio recording of every book
- digital version of every book
- full answer keys

To access video clips, audio tracks and digital books:

1 Go to **www.ladybirdeducation.co.uk**
2 Click "Unlock book"
3 Enter the code below

KkVGLDNwZv

Stay safe online! Some of the DO YOU KNOW? activities ask children to do extra research online. Remember:

- ensure an adult is supervising;
- use established search engines such as Google or Kiddle;
- children should never share personal details, such as name, home or school address, telephone number or photos.